IGoli
EGoli

Poems by
Salimah Valiani

First published in 2024 by
Botsotso
59 Natal St
Bellevue East
Johannesburg 2198
botsotsopublishing@gmail.com
www.botsotso.org.za

ISBN: 978-1-990922-54-1

Acknowledgements:
Versions of some of these poems have appeared in the following publications:
Letter Out: Letter In, Copyright 2009 Salimah Valiani, Inanna Publications;
Praxis Magazine; and Poetry Potion. All works reproduced with permission.

Cover image: Salimah Valiani

Instagram @igoliegoli

Cover, layout and design: Advance Graphics

To the visit to the Women's Prison, Constitution Hill, Johannesburg
that put my life on a new plain.

Author's Note

IGoli, the City of Gold, as Johannesburg is known to the majority in South Africa — is an amalgam of ideals, unknowns, myths, exultancies, swagger, blight, beginnings, rebeginnings. Like all world cities, iGoli is a meeting place: a place of 'original', transnational, subnational, and primordial origins — with no turning back. I explore the amalgam of iGoli in the first part of this collection.

As meeting place, there is no turning back for iGoli, because of eGoli, literally translated from isiZulu as 'within iGoli.' I interpet eGoli as 'that which is underlying', and explore this in the second part of the collection. EGoli, the substrata that defy the apparently finite presented in the first section. Like Pangaea, that changed form and continues to weave and be woven. What Thích Nhất Hạnh calls the 'ultimate dimension', that solves and resolves the 'historical dimension' daily.

Johannesburg and its history of attraction and extraction also offers hints of love, hints of inimba, or empathy, as interpreted broadly by Pumla Gobodo-Madikizela. Love, as I interpret broadly, the only thing to follow from four centuries of taking. Love, as in a restaurant where all within and all wanting entry are blindfolded. Love, as with the tombs of treasure of ancient elites of Mapungubwe, and around the globe — but this time around, for everybody, in life as well as at death.

Contents

IGoli

EGoli

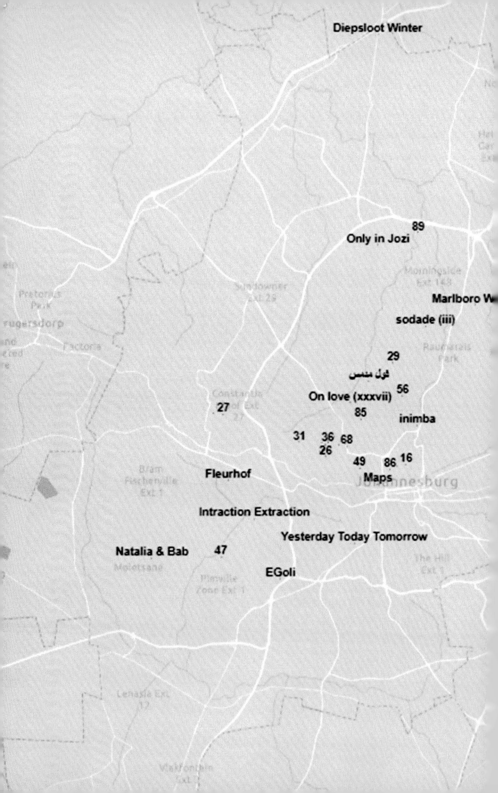

Diepsloot Winter

Only in Jozi 89

Marlboro W

sodade (iii)

29

سمند لوق

On love (xxxvii) 56

85

inimba

31 36 68

26

49 86 16

Fleurhof Maps

Johannesburg

Intraction Extraction

Yesterday Today Tomorrow

Natalia & Bab 47

EGoli

27

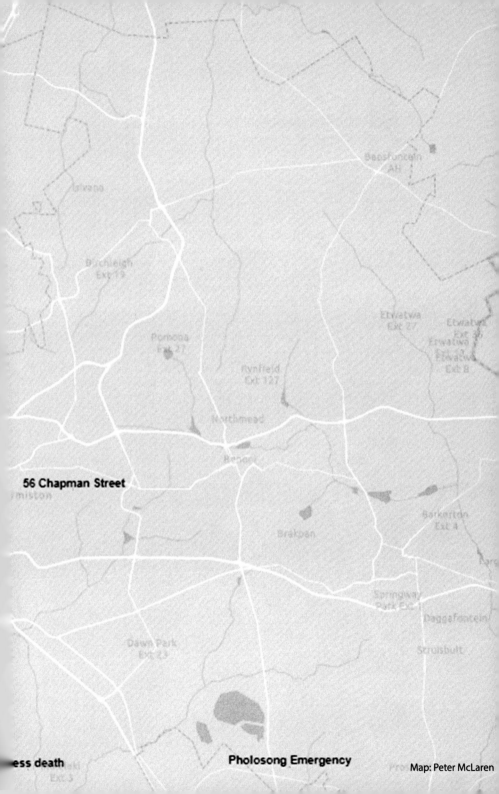

56 Chapman Street

Pholosong Emergency

ess death

Map: Peter McLaren

IGoli

Image: Salimah Valiani

Ndlopfu a yi fi hi rimbambu rin'we.[1]

---

1   Xitsonga proverb: An elephant does not die of a broken rib.

On love (xxxiii)

as with
tiger lilies
all buds
do not
blossom
but like a
red canna
caught
in a ray of
sun
the hope
of the memory
of the hope
that the bud
would blossom
is tall and
red
looming blood star

Dorothy Masuku in Sophiatown 2018[2]

i

I didn't want to sing
singing wanted me
I would think about something
it would come out in song
like when I heard about Patrice Lumumba
I wondered
how does such a big man
just disappear

*

Miriam Makeba used to say
I don't sing about politics
I sing about the truth

*

today as singers
we don't sing about society people's lives though
we are still faced with many issues

we are afraid
worried about making the charts

*

when a young singer asks
Mama I want to cover that song of yours I say
take it it wasn't for me
it was for you

---

2   Italicised words are excerpts from 'In conversation with Dorothy Masuka', held
      at The Mix, Sophiatown Heritage and Cultural Centre, April 20 2018 — possibly
      the last public appearance of Dorothy Masuku.

ii

Miriam Makeba Abigail Khubeka Mary Rabotaba
we are still very close
I see them and we sing together
although I don't go to see them
they come to me
in dreams
for me they are alive as ever

*

I never wanted to return to Rhodesia
it isn't my land
it's just where I was born

iii

Sophiatown was the place
there was none like it
and there never will be one like it again

Re-Map
— after Mbali Mdluli's 2019 Woman of Fire tour

giant girl child dressed in slivers of all semi historical tribes

collectively constructed bright woman on white
patterns surpassing nations

jagged-edged
imbaula-capped
layered lady on a move
invisible
until you need her

pale Victorian plastered flat 70 years back

Ndebele paintings adorning The Market from 2017[3]

towering priestess of broken plates searching for past aesthetics

dykes holding hands in shock of women occupying city space

*

India virgin weave alongside human shit

Pickhandle Mary[4]
regal in Library Square displaced
to grassy square turned
bare

pop star at Bassline
lyric-stamped slenderness damaged more than once
before being removed[5]

---

3   Works of self-taught artist Esther Mahlangu, first made famous in France.
4   Trade union leader, Comrade Fitzgerald, who was also iGoli's first female city
      councillor.
5   Sculpture of Brenda Fassie that is now outside The Market Theatre

*

boxy bronze charging Bree
case and charge in hands

Mama democracy's petrol bomb
dialoguing with child in ichaalo

On love (xxxiv)

child steadied on shoulders
backs stiff
eyes ahead

child in ichaalo
neck tight
staring down

the poster says

lift the child to your heart
let them feel your heart story

spiraling plots
skipping poetics
trip hops
murmuring tensions   tangents
cracks   secret chambers

and learn to know their own

56 Chapman Street

it happens when it happens
once or twice a year

I drive to the shop
buy a bouquet
and throw the flowers to the street

this is for you

*

it was because my gogo insisted that I went to private school
today I am the first PhD of the school

my gogo died before turning 40
younger than I am now

*

I grew up thinking the house was ours

there was a parrot I used to walk around with

likely dispossessing someone in all that ease

the shop where I buy the flowers was owned by Greeks
I used to eat snacks there   pastries rolls

the pastries are still there
now the shop is run by Somalis
people who look more like me

all those who say nothing has changed[6]

---

6   All italics in this collection are voices of Joburgers; used with permission.

Yesterday Today Tomorrow[7]

enter to marimba and djembe

two half-frozen golden mime artists   first sign
of mine workers

two mini-statues other workers at toy train station

tourguides in overalls   boots   cap-lamps

funfair-museum atop former mine

7   English pronouncement of a flowering bush endemic to Brazil, commonly found
     in suburbs of iGoli.

Marlboro Winter

We managed to get through the cold weekend
the loadshedding wasn't too bad
We have an old Beckers anthracite heater
It was my grandfather's from back when we
lived in the CBD
We've been in Marlboro ten years now
The only time you need to open up the heater is to
top up the coal

Diepsloot Winter (pre-loadshedding)

dark evenings
waking early
rejoicing for sun   first things
spotted
all that is fallen   unretrieved
unintended dishevelment of candlelight

endless bending   making tending fire
finding water   warming it
finding food   cooking it   not too much
no refrigeration

Only in Jozi

Zungu Investment
CEPHEID
calibre
Southern Jade Restaurant
GET YOUR BritBox
Ogilvie
13 km World Class Trails
KFC and Pizza Hut at Knightsbridge

Dispossession

in a quaint Haarties market
we bought an Eastern Cape spekboom[8]
carried it home to Jozi

smoothies salads branches
air soil bodies
the spekboom gave and multiplied

we transplanted a branch   outside
the gate   spekboom flourished and was one day
gone

someone stealing back

---

8   Indigenous succulent that nourishes humans and works as a carbon sponge.

Ontvangs B Helen Joseph Hospital

MEMO - ATTENTION ALL PATIENTS
BLACK BAGS GENERAL WASTE
pill boxes
pills
water
I N F O R M A T I O N
entering the system
rush to cure
no appointments
no bills
no money
no doctors
INFECTIOUS WASTE - RED LINER
numbers in a box
Sunday Best
queue from 7
file at 9
doctors at 10
Standing Room Only
casts
crutches
powdered medicine
ointments
self-medication
headlines: Global Sugar Surplus
NON-PENSIONERS PAY HERE
stifling air
body heat

Mammogram Waiting Room Roodepoort

six frames of flowers
plush velvet
filigree cased mirrors
doilies lamps
embroidered drapes
large photo print ladies knitting knee blanket for
Luipaardsviei Old Age Home
caption Mandela Dag/Mandela Day - 18.07.2012

Pholosong Emergency[9]

portrait of the president as you enter
cemented-down plastic chairs
five perfect piles of pamphlets
USE CONDOMS   HAVE PEACE OF MIND   #NO REGRETS

once through the scratchy grey
door with four beige lines to wait on a bed
blue cooler box
SAMPLES FOR LABORATORY
four of seven supply shelves filled
ceiling circle of perforated steel
fluffy grey centre
a sprinkler?
functioning?
periodic *Sorry for the wait*
car crash in Boxburg on a short-staffed Sunday
posted on the wall
The Rule of Nines
an open palm with digits extended
equals one percent of the body's surface area

---

9   Public hospital in Tsakane, a township feeding labour to Johannesburg.

1st Road

Roman warriors tearing African sky
the estate fence greets us
to 1st Road   arrived upon through a few wrong turns

towering fences hiding
luxury homes   glimpses stolen
through gates

at the end of 1st we reach our destination
Hyde Park Corner that always recalls
Manila's remittance malls
super sanitary self-cleaning seats
more than a step up from Rosebank toilets
never visited by Ivorian philosopher Jean now
a Rosebank car guard nor the majority
transferring kombi taxis there

arriving at our only interest in the Corner
Red Chamber not nearly as old as Swallows Inn[10]
white tables
later
an East Asian
a couple mixed race

table talk
deals back operations theatre Cape Town getaways

---

10   Built in the 1940s, in the first Chinatown of iGoli, Swallows Inn is reputed to
     be the oldest Chinese restaurant in (South) Africa.

Inclines

going up
the ways are manifold

slow rising
smooth rising
concrete steps stone
steps studded in glass blocks recycled objects
steppes steeped in green

the real question   what is below

the spread
lifeforms and their density
ratios
the matter of their sustenance

the distance between top and bottom
is a relation
of sight spirit mind

balance comes only with balance

Counterclock Clock

Saturday along a road back to Africa
from the Northern suburbs
after the used car shops
OK Foods
RT Internet
Shoprite Liquor Shop
Curry Den Fast Food and Supermarket
South African Police Service Sophiatown
multicolour boulders

a park teeming with
women children bedsheets swathed in sunbathing clothes

Stop Over Africa
Mm Invest Auto
We Pawn Bikes
Divine Muthi Shop
AMG Halal Takeaway
Bamenda Boy Auto Body
orange pyramids tilted against
red crochet onions
puffy green bushels not grown in Shoprite or Bismillah Supermarket
sweet potatoes half the arm

marrow-thin man writhing to bellowing beats

if you turn the other way
broad avenues
Arthur Matthews Primary School
Baker's Paradise
Gondwana Environmental Solutions
Rhodes Park
McDonalds
Drone Valley
Angelique Koeksusters
Mkonto Manufacturing

Florida Hills Veterinary
West Rand Oncology
Playschool Academy
Chicken Licken
Wheelchairs on the Run
Golf Club Terrace
Florida Fire Station
Modise Computer College
Lexus Security

airbnb Meldene[11]

give me all the succulents
rustic pots
quaint nooks
clever architecture
Neferneferuaten sculpture
Russian novels
antique wood
wind chimes
white candles
indigo clay

when I see the skylight behind
steel diamonds
like stained glass taken to new stained heights I know   this
is not borrowed land

11   In South Africa today, the top 10 percent of the population, some 3.5 million
     people, own 60% of housing, 64% of pension assets, and 99% of stocks/bonds. See
     A. Chatterjee, L. Czajka, A. Gethin, 'A Wealth Tax for South Africa,' Southern Centre
     for Inequality Studies, January 2021.

     Johannesburg is the capital of inequality in South Africa and the African continent
     as a whole.

Meldene to Melville, COVID-19 late third wave

lush lavender
sterling sage
blooming beak orange and velvet magenta
hand jotted sign poised on play chair of dry
broken branches
WE WASH
TEKKIES 70R
BAGS   50R
HATS   30R
pale wheat mooka-kwena flesh[12]
stripped of sulphur-green skin

---

12 Tree found from Kenya to Kwa-Zulu Natal and prominent in the Lowveld of South
    Africa. Pronounced fever tree by Europeans associating it with malaria symptoms
    they were experiencing.

Excess death
or, Acer rubrum[13]

delayed/doubled COVID grant
visit to a friend's
firewater
cracking
prickling
raw and patchy
green scarlet red amber
she didn't
return

---

13 Latin pronouncement of a tree native to northeastern America common in
Johannesburg suburbs.

Westdene Winter
or, Masculinity

think layers of the onion
thin but tenacious   almond/plum/chestnut

thick and ridged   unyielding

slippery film

parts that make us cry the most

think again   Liquidambar tree[14]

resin that flavoured first pipe shared by Emperor Matezuma with
Hernando Cortez

seed hard and burnished   spikes betraying holes

the way the seed changes
umber   burnt sienna   khaki   bronze   bisque
litchi-size to cherry

think again

prickly seed of the London plane tree[15]
mini beige breadfruit
that shrinks

still hanging   or not
for late bloom
soft buff fuzz
only in winter

---

14   Latin pronouncement of a tree commonly found in and around iGoli;
     pronounced sweet gum in English, amberboom in Afrikaans; native to
     southeast and east Asia, the eastern Mediterranean and eastern North America.
15   Widely grown in iGoli and other South African cities, the London plane tree is a
     hybrid said to have happened in 17th century Spain, or London England.

Shrieking yellow

silence
hesitating to speak one's language on a bus

faint yelping
what a child hears inside sounds five walls down

yammering a name
woman who's lost her mother   several siblings   baby thrown to fire

stressing certain syllables
90-year-old matriarch   head of a family of nine
fleeing persecution   third time in two decades

feigned silence
teenage girl raped at home regularly by the boarder

wheezing cries
coal stoves in lungs

shrieking yellow
mine dump mountains

dead silence
gate marked ENTER AT OWN RISK

Fleurhof

hued homes

large   manicured   vegetated   trembling

like the hued hills that tremble and surround[16]

---

16 Fleurhof is one of few suburbs in iGoli boasting immense plots and houses
    where whites are not found. It is also a suburb atop a former mine. Elevated
    levels of lead have been found in soil, adults and children near former
    mines throughout Greater Johannesburg.

Intraction Extraction

I don't know what it is to be enfolded in gold

ask

Silla royals at Gyeongju
who've lived with
gold crowns bells horses
vessels gold silver bronze
gold and silver weapons
stone vessels
20,000 Indo-Pacific blue beads
40,000 artefacts
from 6th century CE

Moche warrior priest at Huaca Rajada
sitting since 3rd century AD in
crescent headdress
gold and silver sceptre
cape of beaten gold
mani(peanut)-shaped gold and silver beads
gold kernels (Sun god/masculinity)
silver kernels (Moon god/femininity)
gold rattles masks 451 noserings earrings textiles feathers

the Tarbagatai mountains
where descendants of the Saka and others roam
among hundreds of body-less
mounds replete with gold
chains plates animals of micro-soldering technique some
2,800 years old

elites of Mapungubwe
ensconced on top of jackal hill among
7,503 ounces of
gold foil covered bowls sceptres animals

copper crafts
glass ostrich eggshell beads

pharaohs lying in multiple caskets of gold and wood at wadi almuluk
among
gold and precious stones
bracelets buckles pendants necklaces
rings scarabs tonics
scarves gloves headdresses
paintings death masks
wine water fruit

I know what it is to be nestled in gold mine dumps

270+ mounds
string of cities on seamsnotstreams
parched footsteps sipping
migrating mine water

On love (xxxv)

how deep can a heart sink

erasure
breathlessness
luminous sea bed

Moon Garden

why are there palms in grasslands
wavering height more visible when a
monumental
parasol   home
of birds
is uprooted to save
a fence

the orchestra is thinner
yard brighter
concrete pool warmer

maybe now
(re)new(ed) blooms
mula-notshi[17] motsantsa[18] uMhlope[19] bushman's pipe[20]

layered ceremony of home

17 Tshivenda pronouncement of an indigenous plant pronounced Forest Elder in
    English.
18 Setswana pronouncement of indigenous plant pronounced Kalahari bauhinia in
    English.
19 isiZulu pronouncement of indigenous plant pronounced Wild Pride of India in
    English.
20 Indigenous plant first pronounced in English by Carl Linnaeus, 1737.

On love (xxxvi)
— after Abel Meeropol

plodding near the Koppies
windfallen magnolia
pumping my palm

flower of 95 million year old tree
native to East Asia Himalayas Americas
pollinated by yet older
beetle that preceded the bee

through to the walk's last leg feet frisking
rose touched lime receptacle warm
as wind is unrelenting

Garnets
or, On love (xxxvii)

they actually grow on trees
not at Pick n Pay

picking is a task
or picking enough

but a picnic on a park trampoline
with just two handfuls

is a taste of the bloody messy rapture of the commons[21]

---

21 Parks and other commons in Johannesburg continue to be well-equipped in
    historically white neighbourhoods, including with fruit trees. This is largely due to
    'Special Ratings Areas' in tax law, that allows people in historically white areas
    to direct tax contributions to neighbourhood upkeep, an aspect of persisting
    inequality in South Africa.

Spirit

full black midcalf skirt
ivory gilet black vines to knees
modest beaded doek
lightly touched lips mouthing words
of an open book
yamanua perambulating the incline[22]
Glascow and 4th

---

22 yamanua: woman of today, in languages of the Andes.

Lower 4th Westdene
or, On love (xxxviii)

voice in the backyard we feel we still hear
absence out front
look up to the roof   you are not there
nimble eyes not
checking shingles chimneys electric fences

Tuesdays we know for sure
crossing the street to fetch the bin
you always delivered
as soon as Pikitup emptied it

when we remember
like you who never forgot
we deliver bins to neighbours

On love (xxxix)

… After the completion of indenture, Indian workers were permitted to buy "preferent" rights to parcels of land in Johannesburg, known as "stands," within a small area widely known as the Coolie Location… On April 8, the authorities razed the Coolie Location by burning it to the ground. The inhabitants, including "1,600 Asiatics, 142 coloured and 1,358 natives," were relocated to a camp 12 miles from the center of Johannesburg, the first step in the evolution of the township later to become known as Soweto.[23]

I'm just a local
from Johannesburg South
I have been to places though
England, Australia, New Zealand, Europe
I'm a pool player
You never hear about pool
But I am the top player in South Africa
I started playing at three my dad taught me
What happened is my dad used to take me to the shebeen
Of course I couldn't reach the table
My dad used to hold me up and I would shoot

My parents supported me a lot
Our uniforms were sponsored air flights
But Iyo! It's expensive
I took R4000 with me to England
I thought it would be enough for a week
I got £150 for it I said What is this?!
But there are those £1 shops there
You can buy gifts lots of gifts

---

23   C. Evans, J. Egan, I. Hall, 'Pneumonic Plague in Johannesburg, South Africa, 1904', Historical Review, Emerging Infectious Diseases, vol. 24, no. 1, January 2018, p. 101.

Natalia Molebatsi and Bab'Themba Mokoena in dance
— after Poetic Thursdays, Soweto Theatre, February 28 2019

she was easy as sunflowers
lacing words with feeling

he warp and weft
visceral strings

exuberance

meditation

we were made of flesh and the blues[24]

we are made from skin and notes

*we were crafted into love and loss and lies many
many times*

we craft ourselves into plains and jungles tundra desert
become one with the cycles

---

24 Italicised words from Natalia Molebatsi's poems that night.

Maps

This is where the Malawians live   the friendliest people
when you go there everyone welcomes you
night or day   you are safe

The Nigerians   No they are fine
talk big but they won't hurt you
theirs is high class crime

No one is like the Zimbabweans
biggest thieves   they will do anything to rob you [25]

where the Malawians live   Fietas
one of South Africa's first three locations
'Malay' location turned mixed with the 1904
razing   of plagued 'Coolie' location
and bursting 'Kaffir' location   never large enough

14th street bazaar   bioscopes   shebeens   cafés   shops
Fietas buzzing bright
drawing the 'white' Vrededorp too
1943 renamed Pageview by Mayor Page
bulldozed '71 when Joburg City remapped Pageview pale
170 merchant families deported from
tattered homes perched on tattered shops
14th street to 30 clicks south   like the rest
Soweto to one side   Lenasia the other

needing some trade for the impaled town
the Department of Community Development built
Oriental Plaza   operating it for years at public loss
a few displaced merchants setting up shop
serving whites arriving in 2300 cars

---

25   Migrants in South Africa compose 0.1% of the country's population, and 0.03%
     of South Africa's prison population. See "Cele: Number of South Africans in
     prisons indicates foreigners are not the problem", Times LIVE, September 12 2022.

inimba[26]

yes it's been a rough morning
I was driving a lady to Killarney
Before crossing over the bridge
I saw a lady walking alone screaming and crying
I said to my passenger Shall we turn back and check on that lady
She said What lady
I told her and she said Oh I was busy on my call
We turned back and found the lady
Now she was really crying
She told us she had been robbed
She was on her way to a new job at the hospital
She had passed her test and it was her first day
The taxi driver missed her stop and told her she just had to walk
up the hill then cross the bridge
I said to my customer Shall we take this lady to work
We dropped her off and then I dropped my customer off
I returned to the hospital and waited an hour
The lady did not come back out
I took a chance because these days they use ladies for funny things
Her pain was so real to me

---

26   Loosely translated from isiXhosa: empathy

On love (xl)

he doesn't leave the house without kissing me
and no one can kiss him after me
his teachers tell him
You are in grade R and you still kissing your mummy!
my father-in-law
he was the same
loved his mummy
would never leave home without kissing her
one day on the highway he remembered and turned back
he told my son
love your mum and everything will work out for you
even him my husband
never leaves the house without kissing his mum
just now when my father-in-law passed away two months ago
we opened the kabr
buried him on top of his mum

On love (xli)

vast tray of violet black gold she
presents modestly
Siyabonga the abundant grocer
thursday to the farm
friday to us in her fly
cherry Cooper
better than
Impala
Fresh Earth
Melville Farmers' Market
not only does she bring
fresh figs marrows heirloom tomatoes
she teaches
kiwano
pearl millet
finger millet
whole red mabele
that bambara nuts are no different to
izidlubu ditloo-marapo phonda tindhluwa nyomo[27]

---

27   isiZulu/isiNdebele, Sesotho, Tshivenda, Xitsonga, and isiShona pronouncements
     of a widely cultivated legume, indigenous to West Africa, where it is pronounced
     bambara nut.

Footsteps

nine years living again in Africa
I've travelled in the south
returned east and north
never west

re-meeting Yves three years after
the start of COVID
who tells me dzidudu
is victory in Ewe
I start hearing how much I've learned of West Africa
living in Jozi
dried cassava strips
revolutionary Guinea via Miriam
kente love
how some Burkinabe women stretch themselves

to be the ends that meet

right here   a way to West Africa
deepening encounters in iGoli

inimba (ii)

I'm writing a book too
about my story
I was living in that school corner of Thornton and 4th
my parents were the caretakers
The principal saw something in me
wanted to give me a chance
he asked my parents if I could live with his family
I learned Afrikaans
did very well through postsecondary
The principal took me everywhere with the family
stood by me even as his friends scorned my presence
He lost friends
It wasn't political
He says he was doing what he needed to

On love (xlii)

Do you all have papers?
They are checking at Rosebank
No we must protect you
We are here We eat Everyday Because of you
You are our brothers and sisters

Sizwile turned back to Diepsloot for her passport[28]
rebegan the trip

but didn't need it
the next taxi driver took the back roads

---

28 Sizwile is the isiNdebele pronouncement of the emotion pronounced 'I have had
    enough' in English.

iSothamilo[29]
or, On love (xliii)

my first encounter with it
walking fast
Maboneng to town
with fiercely internationalist Zulu friend
far east on Commissioner
before Troyeville
a hollow complex ringing with Fanakalo
liquid orange language
created in the mines   heated crossroads of the
country Southern slice and more
aspiration of Esperanto born and living through
needs of unintending magnates

second
participant observer transcribed Fanakalo phrases
first depiction of women's lives in the mines[30]

third
Dudula [Dubula] in Alexandra
lover sharing how Fanakalo is ridiculed rejected
child throttling truth of the present and tumbling
back of another friend's words
*if you had seen how my Tswana mother was made to feel in our Pedi
community*

xth
skayf/kunhavigi
Fanakalo/Esperanto for
share
remaking everything

---

29 isiZulu pronouncement of the concept pronounced 'humanity' in English.
30 See Asanda Benya, 'Women in mining: occupational culture in the making', PhD
   Thesis, University of the Witwatersrand, 2016.

big little forest

yellow white purple
floating off the koppie

sun pacifying dark fruits

golden herb patching red black yellow white

towering poisonous mushrooms stubby umbrellas cone hats

cheetah trunk sitting trunk leaf frill skirted

weaving branches

nutty fruit

owl rock tilting with wind
proliferating lightness

On love (xliv)

how many ways to say share

greater than the sum of

languages
nuances
hybrid languages
songs
acts
beings

EGoli

Image: Phumi Mtetwa

518 taxa (species and lower ranks) in 298 genera and 84 families occur on the Melville Koppies Ridge. 464 are indigenous taxa, 54 are alien taxa. Of the indigenous vegetation, most are forbs, perennials, resprouters after fire, mesic and autotrophs. Of the alien taxa, most are forbs, perennials, resprouters after fire, mesic and autotrophs.[31]

31   W. Ellery, K. Balkwill, K. Ellery, R. Reddy, 'Conservation of the Vegetation on the Melville Ridge, Johannesburg', African Journal of Botany, 2001, vol. 67, p. 263.

Letsopa le kgobja le sa le metse, la oma le hlaba.[32]

32 Sepedi proverb: Clay is taken out while it's still soft; allowed to dry, it begins
to prick.

or, Only in Jozi (ii)
or, On love (xlv)

فول مدمس [33]

downtown Montreal you used to eat فول
at Basha's student rate

then in London for breakfast with
Widad and small daughter escaped
from Sudan   chilli powder and salt
small piles on the side

years later Marianne raving
how they serve it like her Armenian mums with
fresh tomatoes parsley spring onion
in the Lebanese grocery near Little Italy Ottawa

only in Jozi
at Cafe Liban
after reading how Rahul relished fūl in Tigray picked up
somewhere in Egypt[34]

did you feel all this

---

33 In Latin script, fūl mudammas.
34 From Elleni Centime Zeleke's piece, 'The Enemy in Her Imagination: A Fable',
    Chimurenga, June 9 2021.

Origins

land(s)

it was Golda
mother of Sophy   not Herman
who brought the first piano to town
Golda's daughter's husband sold the land
became known as the founder of Sophiatown[35]

*

a few stone age artefacts
of Batswana nomads
remain in the Melville Koppies[36]

labour

from Cornwall tin to Benoni coal
many miners came some settled their legacy in names
Baragwanath John Barag started the department store
some sailed home
after large numbers began dying the white death[37]

*

John Nkadimeng
trade unionist liberationist ambassador to Cuba
never knew his father Bap'Mahudu
Pedi migrant worker in the Witwatersrand mines early 1900s
who contracted silicosis and died after a month-long
donkey journey home

---

35 This verse and other biographical verses based on excerpts from a display at the Apartheid Museum.
36 See R. Mason, 'The Prehistoric People of Melville Koppies,' in Melville Koppies Nature Reserve, Guidebook, The Johannesburg Council for Natural History, 1984, pp 19-24.
37 Early 20th century colloquial term for silicosis

capital

the battery system workers for cattle via
recruiters and chiefs
when the workers had complaints
workers from British West Africa via Belgian Congo helped
them write English letters to compound managers[38]

*

These whitish rocks are quartz
signs there is gold in the vicinity
Leopold Reinecke came with seam tracking technology
and knew how to use it
passing the information to Goldfields
He considered this insider knowledge
and refused Goldfields' shares[39]

*

largest dry port in the world
prehistorically an ocean floor
futuristically a dry island amid rising seas
or melding into acid mine water[40]

38 From a tour guide's talk at the Workers' Museum, June 5 2019, Newtown. See also
     B. Yates, 'The Origins of Language Policy in Zaire', The Journal of Modern African
     Studies, vol. 18, no. 2, pp 257-279.
39 As told by Reinecke's great grandson, Luke Hutchison, March 20, 2022.
40 From Holding Water, a multidisciplinary exploration of Johannesburg
     commissioned by POOL and the Oceanic Humanities for the Global South, Wits
     Institute for Social and Economic Research.

metsi/amanzi/emanti/mvura/madzi/ruwa/water/জল/l'eau/ᨊᨛ [41]

below the Limpopo
death a one-way escalator
the living of all tongues
burying dead one
atop
another
pressing
down
deep
deeper
till the ocean of numbing
and the ocean of unrelease
meet

---

41 Pronouncements that have migrated to iGoli over the centuries.

Down Main Street, Melville
or, Umsebenzi

non-public post office
gone used book shop
plantain fufu
coriander sausages handmade steak pasty
সাধের লাউ sprawling spaza wall[42]
fine macrame in rough cotton cream some
with beads slightly soiled bush hung in traffic circle
to keep me in iGoli

---

42   sadher lau in Latin script; Bengali pronouncement of a vegetable pronounced
      calabash/bottle gourd in English. A folk song sings: সাধের লাউ liberated me/its
      flesh fed my bones/I made a drum of its shell and nourished my spirit.

Umsebenzi (ii)

untangle me
here
don't
twist me up more
throw me out
entangle me
leave me
dangling
knot me up
topspinning strings
translucentcapiztoruggedseadump

Footsteps (ii)

we live behind the eucalyptus curtain[43]

but we want to leave

our daughter will be a teenager soon
we don't want to be helicopter parents

accompanying her to parties
hiding behind park bushes when she's meeting friends

always worrying about what could happen

I am from the Vaal
my husband is from Rexdale
big Somali community there

but we wouldn't go to Toronto
COVID is crazy over there

---

43 Though part of water scarce grasslands where trees are few, Johannesburg is one
of the world's largest urban forests. Throughout the 19th century, European
settlers imported seeds to plant trees. With the discovery of gold, eucalyptus
trees were grown in and around the city to provide wooden props for
underground mines. Often referred to as gum trees, eucalyptus grow fast but
require plenty of water.

Where will we go?
— after Reuben Caluza, Philip Miller and Tshegofatso Moeng's 'Wa Q'um uDalimede'

acapella of
maxis minis
waist coats culottes top hats
black patent emerald
umDoni[44] indigo
litchi sky

      that splits

                       four
                       five
                       nervy pitches
                       bungled baritones
                       wavering
                       crackling
                       claps
                       seven
                       kneeslaps
                       throaty triggers
                       chesty blasts

iGoli party 1924 just before Industrial Conciliation Act

---

44 Indigenous fruit of Kwa Zulu Natal, Zimbabwe and Mozambique, brewed to treat respiratory diseases in humans. The tree leaves are eaten by kudus. When the tree is sometimes infested with caterpillars, these are eaten by crowned hornbills and other birds.

RosesRunways

runway roses the first thing to greet me

second *If you want to mine in Zambia FNB is here to help*

third delele[45]
katapa[46]   kalembla[47]
ondwe impua[48]
kapenta[49] ntwilo[50] nshima[51]
entire cooking lesson from a simple question

fourth Oliver Tambo House

*

of mounds of jewellery I packed only copper
spirits of maimed miners water land moving my hands

*

placard chiming
when the mining finishes   what will we have to show

soil chiming 25 mushroom species
tangy tomatoes roses

---

45 Nyanja pronouncement of a vegetable pronounced okra/lady finger in English.
46 Nyanja pronouncement of a vegetable known as cassava leaves in English.
47 Nyanja pronouncement of a vegetable known as sweet potato leaves in English.
48 Nyanja pronouncement of a vegetable of the brinjal family, English
     pronouncement nonexistant.
49 Nyanja pronouncement of a fish pronounced Lake Tanganyika sardine in English.
50 Nyanja pronouncement of a nut pronounced groundnut in English.
51 Nyanja pronouncement of a vegetable pronounced maize in English.

On love (xlvi)
or, Umsebenzi (iii)

Yes that's us
We are here driving for Bolt

What I miss most about Venda?
Rainy days
My gogo used to roast peanuts
and make us kids sit in a circle in the kitchen
She would tell us riddles
and when we solved the riddle
she would give us a handful of peanuts

દારમ[52]

sitting on pomegranate-velour throne
in her public housing apartment downtown Calgary
1972 Uganda refugee
peeling દારમ gifting us with juicy gems

[53]अनर انار انار

40 years on in one of Africa's pomegranate heartlands
I learn from a friend's facebook
the art of peeling انار
cutting cross down from rose leather crown

cross my heart she said
anaar is my favourite

ગુલાબ mapera[54]

walking in Westdene to visit a friend
my daughter-lover-of-pomegranates spots
a pomegranate tree

unseen before so close to home

recalling my parents spotting ગુલાબ mapera on the drive to Hana
I say fetch a stick

first time they'd seen them since 1950s East Africa
climbing car roof   tapping branches
rose-flavour riches falling into

---

52 daram in Latin script, Gujarati pronounciation of a fruit pronounced
    pomegranate in English.
53 anar in Latin script; from right to left, Farsi, Urdu and Hindi pronouncements of a
    fruit pronounced pomegranate in English.
54 gulab mapera in Latin script; literally, rose guava in Gujarati mixed with Swahili;
    English pronouncement non-existent.

praying palms

kgaranata umHalinadi[55]

via Rotterdam
the world buys many from South Africa

but a handful of South Africans I've met know
the pomegranate grew up eating it

one said there were trees in every second house where
his gogo worked he and his friends ate plenty of kgaranata
but when he left he stopped seeing them

the way my નાનીમા's apartment[56]
was sold to private developers
umHalinadi is not for the majority
multi-gem fruit following routes flowing out

---

55 Sepedi and isiZulu pronouncements of a fruit pronounced pomegranate in
    English.
56 nanima in Latin script; Gujarati pronounciation of mother's mother; English
    pronounciation non-existent.

Wealth[57]

five sounds of 't'
two sounds of 'k'
four click sounds
how many sounds does your language make

twenty consonants six vowels forty-five sounds four thousand
characters...
can we say the more letters characters sounds tones
the more richness and subtlety accommodated within

within what
a language culture people
and the shared places of many peoples
metropolis country world cosmos

where do we meet and how
who attempts first to make unfamiliar sounds

do we meet at all
if not why not

twenty letters ten sounds six clicks a thousand characters...
how many worlds does your tongue embrace

---

57 This poem was first published in Dear South Africa, the first section of my
collection, Letter Out: Letter In (Inanna 2009), inspired by the year I lived in Cape
Town. Letter Out: Letter In was also the beginning of the suite of love poems that
continued in subsequent collections and seems unstoppable.

Recipe
or, Wealth (ii)

ibohlololo[58]
honey-lime
elephant gray
grasslands sun
tangy
tart
spritzing
crunch
iGoli eGoli festival of seeds
enkomamawanga[59]
monyaku[60]
tozalin[61]
galagadeya[62]

---

58 isiZulu pronouncement of an indigenous flower pronounced baby sun rose in English.
59 Luganda pronouncement of a fruit indigenous to Central Asia; pronounced pomegranate in English.
60 Sepedi pronouncement of a vegetable indigenous to Southern Africa; pronounced African cucumber in English.
61 Hausa pronoucement for a seed indigenous to North America; pronounced sunflower in English.
62 Chichewa pronouncement of a fruit indigenous to Paraguay, northeast Argentina and Brazil; pronounced granadilla in South African English.

On love (xlvii)
  — after Timothy Moloi's 'Always & Forever' commemorating
    Luther Vandross, Joburg Theater 2016

lime green teepees fusing
yellow stars throughout

blue sun rays dewy purple soil

green threaded cylinders
bubbles whirling

white fumey velvet

golden waves

dizzy proud loops

map puzzling heart chambers

sodade (iii)
or, Joy of Jazz Sandton 2017
            — for Shereen Mills

mid-twentieth century
Ma left her Ma
two continents behind
no letters no phones

early twenty-first
I left Ma
same two continents
opposite direction
near instant means of communication

similar mainsprings
different cycles
same longings

the way Salif Keita strums a high G
and Selaelo Selota strums a high E

Mushrooms in Mint
or, On love (xlviii)
            — for Myesha Jenkins (1948-2020)

still bringing us together
two and a half years on
Tuesday poets what's app group you created for
Myesha's Memoirs podcasting our
poetry and jazz to celebrate
your life
soon to end

Jozi House of Poetry
where we first met
at the Bioscope where you started it
and chose to move to Afrikan Freedom Station
when Maboneng became too lit

Out There Sessions you spawned at The Orbit
adding a new instrument   stanzas
to valves reeds and keys
featuring so many poets musicians
rarely yourself

you and a few springing
Feelah Sistah! Collective
poets still backstage early 21st century Africa
Soft fists...
Heaving the needles
as Plath once wrote[63]

how in Laughter Remembered you rendered
the poetry of a young girl's fierce hug raw truth

---

63   From 'Mushrooms', in The Colossus and Other Poems, by Sylvia Plath, 1961.

unfurling art for humanity in schools branching beyond
the choice few
to South Africa's many languages
spoken written drawn

mushrooms that first appeared in my mint patch
day after you passed
orange on green yesterday
white on green today
What are you doing out so late, ma?
you once wrote
mushrooms in mint
you answer now
like stanzas and jazz

Footsteps (iii)

how often you noted
the way African sons
become estranged never returning home

Adnan who didn't meet his father again[64]
Abdulai and the daughter he left[65]
Emmanuel lost on the other side of the continent[66]
Tariro returning home to die[67]
Kilmi in the train twenty years on turning away when you said his
name[68]

how you began wondering is this a riff of Africa and its
never-ending diaspora and one day caught it pulsing
your soles

---

64 Adnan: popular name of Morocco, meaning settler/to stay; pre-Islamic legendary
     figure.
65 Abdulai: popular name of Senegal, meaning 'servant of Allah'.
66 Emmanuel: popular name of Haiti, meaning 'God is with us'.
67 Tariro: popular name of Zimbabwe, meaning hope/looking to the future.
68 Kilmi: popular name of Somalia, meaning intelligence.

Distances

a doorway and mirror can lead to
a window but only if sitting

the view   weaver leaving a wall that is cracked and splitting

you knew it would come
but not how

the strain of making contact
near and far failing

getaway like never before

finally making contact
meeting weariness lining eyelids kneecaps muscle
you take it in blink
paralysed heart down   your body still moving

referral nurse ambulance
maybe a bed tests

you wish you could be there with those you wish
did not have to be alone footing the wall

instead you are here
seated before a doorway
watching the space a weaver has left

Only in Jozi (iii)

Raul said in London
when I made વગારેલા છોબા[69]
it was the best of mine he'd tasted
that his mum in Mexico would fry eggs in sauce like mine

24 years seven more cities I try mastering those eggs

only in Jozi
with Mzansi lover of Ecuador
do I succeed

---

69 Kachhi/Gujarati dish of tomato fried rice; wagarela chokkha in Latin Script.

**Greenhill Grocer
or, On love (xlix)**

tucked among
raw mangos
curry leaves
Durban methi
sugar bean pods
coconut cubes
kumquats
drumsticks
umbili
garlic shoots
green bananas
tofu
I see
glassy red
glistening wrap
impossible first crunch
just like forty years
four countries
ago

Only in Jozi (iv)
or, On love (l)

strips of cloth woven on horizontal looms   sewn together
kente
dates back to the 11th century

the prerogative of men
a single strip can take three months to weave

*

a 17th century European noted a hene taking apart silk[70]
to weave silk threads into kente

original kente was made of indigo-hued
homegrown cotton

*

Adinkra is the Asante system of symbols that speaks the kente
through Adinkra people understand statements of the wearers

toku kra toma   pattern commemorating Queen Mother Toku
executed in battle mid-18th century

adweneasa   my skill is exhausted
every motif different   to please the hene

sika futoro   gold dust
precolonial medium of exchange

akyem pem   thousands of women and men
who defended the Asante kingdom

---

70   hene: Asante king.

nyankon-ton   God's eyebrow
celebrating the rainbow

*

Ewe kente is plain weaving with motifs
maybe because the Ewe did not have a monarchy

animals and objects hinting at model conduct

no one follows the elephant in the bush and gets wet from morning dew

crocodiles do not drown in a river no matter how deep

crabs   determination

birds   merriment

punctual butterflies

versatile chameleons

gecko   silence

*

Ewe kente has yellow green pink purples blue oranges
Asante kente has orange gold greens white black

it is hard to make a distinction between Asante and Ewe kente
of the early twentieth century and before

*

everyone had a right to kente
anyone who could afford to have it made

Kwame Nkrumah wore kente encouraging all to wear it
offering it to international guests

*

kente weaver at the opening
of a small kente exhibit in Braam
rising from the audience
gifting the white USAmerican lecturer
Mzansi and Ghana colours woven in kente

Fidel Castro at Lillisleaf Farm 2017[71]
or, On love (li)

i

The first time I spent an extended time with Fidel
he asked me How many math teachers are allocated to Limpopo?

and

How many litres of petrol are consumed in South Africa each year?

When we marched in a demonstration together he disputed
the estimated turnout He had worked out the number of people
in our vicinity and the area we had walked...

*

I was born in 1959
In the first ten years of our revolution there were daily challenges
We tried our best
But what kept us going was the speech by Fidel every week
Assessing the situation and giving us ideas on how to engage

*

Gabriel Garcia Marquez had a habit of showing Fidel drafts
of his novels One was Chronicle of a Death Foretold
Fidel read it and when Marquez asked his impressions he said
It's good... But there is one mistake
The guy with the machine gun who is shooting... It's impossible
Either change the angle or the distance between him and the...

---

71 Inspired by the spirit, if not precise forms, of interventions made at the Centenary
Commemoration of Fidel Castro Ruz, November 4, 2017. Lillisleaf Farm is a
museum in current day Johannesburg built on a farm formerly used by under-
ground anti-Apartheid activists.

ii

We were working in Santiago de Cuba
There was an old woman who had been a slave
Fidel said it was crucial that she be given the opportunity
to read and write So that she could talk about her experience
And it could become a known part of our history

*

He was a man with the power to mobilise an entire nation
In a year and three months he convinced the students to abandon
their studies their comforts of the city all that they knew
to go to the countryside and teach literacy
These were children of the middle classes
He convened them to contribute
This is what we must preserve in Cuba
The means by which Cubans today can contribute to the world

*

I am one of several NUM members who went to Cuba
to study engineering in the 1990s
I returned to South Africa and have worked many
mining engineer positions since
That is radical economic transformation

iii

It was 1983 just three weeks before the USA assassinated
Prime Minister Maurice Bishop We were in Grenada for the
All African Students Convention We saw the impact of Fidel
and Cuba on the Grenadians and on Maurice Bishop
We used to say Behind every tree is a Cuban

*

Cuba the small island nation had the courage to stand up to
imperialism and capitalism To make the choice
of socialism over barbarism as Rosa Luxemburg put it

*

Illiteracy was wiped out in Cuba in nine months
This was done largely by candlelight
We said we would do it in South Africa in five years
Today we are still sitting with this challenge

*

I wish we could have a school of selflessness here in South Africa
I will never forget what I learned from being part of the
movement for the ALBA started by the late comrade Chavez
We gathered many times in la Havana to build this vision
cooperation based on indigenous principles and practices
Cuba put a lot into this movement

*

On the school of selflessness
It was in the camps in our guerrilla struggle
But we don't want to say it is possible in South Africa
only in times of war

After the launch of Cradles
or, ሚጣሚጣ 2018
or, On love (lii)

to the one end
Manel of Bulgaria Sri Lanka Canada with
Mzansi-USAmerican Namane
cradling our toddlers
prancy and buzzing like no one was watching and this wasn't
Little Addis in Maboneng
to the other end
Cuban doctors and musician
Spanish layering English
laughter and intensity nearly charged as the toddlers'
South African and other feminists in the middle
discussing the womb
rarely recognised first cradle
and the irreplicable cradle of Cuban revolutionary healthcare
right-flanking the feminists
domestic worker and friend enjoying a meal not tried before
and likely not since
gathering to be savoured
like pre-COVID injera
teff never so available again

sodade (iv)

loss felt by two
who were three
the same loss felt by ten
who were thirteen

because the vacuity of space emptied
is different to the bareness
of one that was always one

the way Lorraine Klassen singing Miriam and Thandi in 2019
is different to Tu Nokwe singing her journals with a nod to Princess
Magogo[72]

or how a drum set replacing so many drummers is different to
a guitar strumming its strings into song

---

72 Tu Nokwe studied at the Manhattan School of Music, and later composed
    Inyakanyaka, an album based on journals she kept in New York, combined with
    her tribute to songwriter and Zulu royal, Princess Magogo.

EGoli
or, On love (liii)

Saturdays when Auntie used to come to Kwa Thema[73]
after a day of tennis with Mama
around this time we would sit together
the police would come and demand a pass
beat her for not being in Geluksdal[74]

but the beating did not start with the destruction of Payneville
still said to have been done
to alleviate the overcrowded conditions…
create more congenial living conditions
for the black industrial workers while noting
Blacks numbered 99 300 Asians 1 200 Coloureds 1 500[75]

Auntie was one of those who said
If I feel for boerewors I must be able to queue for boerewors
If I feel for curry I can go to that queue and if I want
pap en vleis I should be able to queue there

and the other workers agreed

after training at Baragwanath
Auntie never worked as a nurse again[76]

*

---

73 Township built for black Africans at the edge of the white town, Springs, known
as die laaste dorpie, Afrikaans for the last town on the Johannesburg gold seam.

74 Township built for mixed race Africans at the edge of Springs.

75 Like Sophiatown and many others, Payneville was initially a multi-ethnic town.
For the official history of why it was dismantled, see 'Springs - History of a Gold
Town' on facebook.

76 For a brief history of nurses resisting apartheid see 'An historical overview of
nursing struggles in South Africa', October 1988, South African History Online.

1958 best time of my life
We were at our best in the 50s
We would wake up in the morning and just feel happy
It was home sweet home
No news of this person dying that one stabbed

On days off or after duty we would wash up and get ready
We were the best dressed Especially the men!
Their black and white or black and brown shoes
Dressing up was to please yourself
And respect others

We would meet up with Miriam Makeba Angie Kubeka
Father Trevor Huddleston who gave me Cry the Beloved Country
and Father Jeremy Kerr

I was in love with a Chinese boy puppy love
no demands or expectations
Evenings after enjoying Jonas Gwanga and others
he would accompany me home
two trains and a taxi to Uncle Charlie's
Back at Bara by 7pm when the doors shut

I am old now
I'll never forget that town
Sophiatown was a place for everyone
We didn't even know it was apartheid
no discrimination interrogation harassment
a culture of love

On love (liv)
— after Mansions of the Moon, by Shyam Selvadurai,
and a dream in Magliesburg

along Table Mountain's feet
umnayamanzi[77]
parasols that harboured me
when I first landed

19 years on   diaphanous   you come to visit
East African rift to Cape Fold via Rockies and Rio
Grande rift

acacia seed necklet gifted
to Yasodhara by Rupasiri
farewell at a foot of the Himalayas

when Yasodhara reached home
to greet her parent
like I didn't
Pamita said *I have now passed to another world*
in which pain and death are my greatest reality
and I understood your final silence

six trunks braiding up a foot of the Magaliesburg
fine vine green climbing the centre
rhizomes resting beneath
surfacing at times to visit

---

77 isiXhosa pronouncement of a tree pronounced acacia in English. The African
acacia climbing Table Mountain is also pronounced Nyanga flat top in English. The
dome-shaped acacia, or Mokala tree is the most recognizable tree in the Kalahari
desert. For thousands of years, nomads throughout Africa relied on acacias for
territorial organisation, spiritual practice and law. The acacia's tap root can reach
60 metres down, allowing the tree to access deep ground water. As such, the tree
can rehabilitate land, while growing 20 metres tall.

Acknowledgements

This collection, in this form, would not have been possible without Phumzile Mtetwa, my heartspiritmate and principal sounding board. My sense of the heartbeats of iGoli, as presented here, would not have become conscious without the sharings of Auntie Samelia, Maleeah, Victor, Nozuko, Mum Regina, Sivu, MaDre, Frank, Naomi, Shereen, Somar, Sha, Maia, Ralph, Jeffrey, Mandla, Dan, Manel, Namane, Sari, Silvia, Jehad, Kenneth, Sis Lindi, Lydia, Yousuf, Zaide, Charlie, Mahmud, Muneer, the Greeff's, Luke, Guruji Saradindu, Siya, imbomba, and countless near strangers that all form my Jozi family. Without Peter, the mapped poems at the start of the collection would not have been possible. Without Lydia, the poetry and bread would not flow and rise as they do for me in iGoli. In its entirety, my creative oeuvre would not have expanded as it has without the backing of my Ma, Zebunnisha Nanjuwany, who has tended — in spite of her own needs — my mitshimbilo (Tshivenda: disease of the wanderers) which has thus far proven to be unstoppable.

Salimah Valiani is a poet, activist, and researcher born in the city first named Mohkinstsis, by the Blackfoot First Nation. Like her mother, of Mitala Maria, Uganda, and her father, of Bukoba, Tanzania, she left her birth home as a young adult. Her journey of study, work, and living has included extended stops in Montreal, London, New York City, Binghamton, Toronto, Cape Town, Ottawa, and Johannesburg. Beyond books, she has authored a range of articles and policy papers on North/South inequality, development, health/care, and global economic justice.

Books by Salimah Valiani

Poetry

Love Pandemic (audio and print, Daraja Press 2022)
29 leads to love (Inanna Publications 2021)
Dear South Africa, (Praxis Magazine Chapbook Series 2019)
Cradles (Daraja Press 2017)
land of the sky (Inanna Publications 2016)
Letter Out: Letter In (Inanna Publications 2009)
breathing for breadth (TSAR Publications 2005)

Research

The Africa Care Economy Index (UNDP and FEMNET 2022)
The Future of Mining in South Africa: Sunset or Sunrise?
(MISTRA 2018)
Rethinking Unequal Exchange - The Global Integration of Nursing Labour Markets (University of Toronto Press 2012)

Image: Ibrahim Stein